Flowers
from your
Garden

For Alan

Flowers
from your
Garden

Edith Brack

Illustrated by Susan Claypole White

THE NATIONAL TRUST

UNWIN HYMAN
London   Sydney

First published in Great Britain by Unwin Hyman,
an imprint of Unwin Hyman Limited, 1987.

Published in association with The National Trust
for Places of Historic Interest or Natural Beauty

UNWIN HYMAN LIMITED
Denmark House, 37–39 Queen Elizabeth Street
London SE1 2QB
and
40 Museum Street
London WC1A 1LU

Allen & Unwin Australia Pty Ltd
8 Napier Street, North Sydney, NSW 2060,
Australia

Allen & Unwin New Zealand Pty Ltd
with the Port Nicholson Press
60 Cambridge Terrace, Wellington, New Zealand

British Library Cataloguing in Publication Data
Brack, Edith
    Flowers from your garden.
    1. Plants, ornamental   2. Flower gardening
    3. Flower arrangement
    I. Title   II. National Trust
    635.9   SB404.9

ISBN 0–04–440047–0

Designed by **Elizabeth Palmer**
Typeset by **Latimer Trend & Company Ltd,
Plymouth**
Printed in Great Britain by
William Clowes Ltd, Beccles & London

Contents

Introduction

Writing a book of this size about any aspect of gardening is like trying to put a quart into a pint pot. There is so much to say—it is a case of wondering what to leave out as much as wondering what to put in.

I feel sure I was destined to be a gardener. For as long as I can remember I have been totally captivated by all things that grow. The sheer magic of it all has never paled and I hope it never will. I marvel at the diverse shapes of the flowers, the delicacy and colouring of the petals, the ingenuity of the pollination process and the infinite variety of leaf forms. Have you noticed how every leaf seems to be just the right shape to accompany its flower? It is something I never cease to marvel at and when I am arranging flowers, only on rare occasions do I substitute a leaf from another plant, although I may, and often do, enhance them with different foliage.

In this book I have tried to encompass as varied a selection as space allows of plants, shrubs and trees to enjoy throughout the seasons of the year.

My choice to a great extent has been influenced by another interest—flower arranging, although I consider myself to be a gardener first and foremost. Some of the more unusual plants beloved by the plantsman are not included because they do not hold the same interest for me as they have no flower arranging possibilities.

I hope, however, I have included some of the less well-known plants which might be new to you whilst mentioning many old favourites. As well as writing about the plants themselves I have included various ideas for flower arrangements along with tips for conditioning, drying and preserving plant material.

If this book will inspire you to grow something new, or even tempt you to experiment more with your flower arranging then I, for one, will be delighted.

Spring

There is something about spring in the garden that has its own particular magic. Maybe it is the anticipation of things to come which gives this air of excitement and even the knowledge that there may be disappointments around the corner cannot dim this heightened expectation.

For most people the arrival of spring is trumpeted by the daffodils, surely designed by nature for this purpose. Botanically they are all narcissi and the Royal Horticultural Society's classified list contains about eight-thousand cultivated varieties. They cannot all be mentioned but here are a few which are well worth considering.

Dwarf narcissi are great favourites on the rock garden as well as in the border where they do well even in the more exposed places. Highly recommended is 'February Gold' with its clear yellow petals and trumpet and 'Jack Snipe', with white petals and a yellow trumpet, both are listed in the *Cyclamineus* species division. 'April Tears' bears four or five little corn-yellow flowers on a stem, and 'Silver Chimes' also carries several flowers on a stem, but those which have pure white petals with a pale primrose cup belong to the *Triandrus* group. Moving on to the more popular everyday daffodil, two particular favourites are 'Golden Harvest' and 'Carlton' which come up year after year in their golden finery. Others which never fail to please are 'Mount Hood' and 'Cantatrice' both of which are of the palest cream colour. Especially appealing are the double varieties, like 'Irene Copeland' with its camellia-like flowers with petals in two shades of cream, and 'Double Event' with white and lemon-yellow petals. 'Cheerfulness' is probably the most popular of the *Poeticus* group with its two or three sweetly-scented blooms of cream and yellow.

All narcissi when cut last better in shallow water because of the cellular structure of their stems, so it is best to arrange them on a pinholder or using new floral foam made especially for spring flowers. Daffodils usually look better arranged more or less as they grow, just a few grouped together with their own leaves on a sliver of wood or in a basket with a

9

few branches of forsythia for example. Even if the forsythia is not yet in flower in the garden, you can still use it in your arrangements. Cut a few branches while they are still in tight bud and place them in warm water, in a warm situation and they will soon open up. Double narcissi are much more sophisticated–looking flowers and benefit from more elegant designs. But dwarf narcissi can look delightful displayed in a plate garden. It is easy to do. Simply fill a pretty dish with moss and in it secrete one or two small containers for your flowers. If you like, a small twig can be added to give extra height to your arrangement and a few shiny pebbles for extra interest. Other spring bulbs such as *Chionodoxa, Crocus, Muscari* and

Scillas can be very successfully shown this way. This idea can be extended as a lovely way to enjoy a clump of primroses or polyanthus, although in this case the whole root can be brought in and hidden beneath the moss and when the flowers die off it can be popped back into the garden for next year.

After daffodils, tulips are undoubtedly the most popular spring bulb and, again, there is a bewildering collection of species, varieties and hybrids but, unlike the narcissi, they do not always go on flowering year after year. There are single and double tulips, peony-flowered and lily-flowering, exotic parrot and fringed tulips, with frilly edged petals as well as the multi-coloured Rembrandt tulips. Then there are the

species tulips for naturalizing which can be left undisturbed from one year to another. Two of these which put up a marvellous show every year in the garden are the *Tulipa tarda* which opens wide in the spring sunshine with star-like brightness and *Tulipa praestans* 'Fusilier', with two or three flaming scarlet flowers to each stem.

Each year, treat yourself to a few out-of-the-ordinary tulips purely for flower arranging as it is always a thrill to see them flower for the first time. Try 'Spring Green', which may sound more like a cabbage than a delightful viridiflora tulip! It has a beautiful head of ivory, green and cream. Another new variety, a parrot tulip named 'Estella Rijnveld', has very flashy white and raspberry-red, deeply laciniated and waved petals. Both were ideal flowers for using in eye-catching modern designs.

Tulips in general are difficult flowers to arrange because they have a mind of their own and their stems can twist and even grow in the water after they have been arranged, but if they are arranged *en masse* this idiosyncracy can be lessened.

Hyacinths are the last of the three types of bulbs traditionally associated with spring and have a glorious perfume. To stand by a bed of them in the evening when the scent of the flowers is always intensified, is pure delight. This is why, no doubt, so many are grown indoors.

Like many other flowers, hyacinths look better grown in groups of self colours rather than in straight lines. They are ideal for planting in pots and urns or even old chimney pots as features in the spring garden which later can be replanted with fuchsias and geraniums. Here are the names of one each of the colours which give particular pleasure: 'L'Innocence' (white), 'City of Haarlem' (yellow), 'Lady Derby' (pink), 'Jan Bos' (red), 'Cote d'Azure (sky blue) and 'Concorde' (royal blue). If you do want to pick a few from the garden, be sure to leave behind a piece of stem and a few leaves to nourish the bulb for next year.

Hyacinths are charming at the centre of a spring basket of flowers but care is needed as the bottom of the stems tend to splay out when put in water. If you wish to impale them on a pinholder wrap some raffia around the base of

Parrot Tulip

the stem before doing so, but if pushing them into floral foam, it will be much easier if you first insert a drinking straw up the stem.

A particularly dramatic spring flower is the camellia an exotic-looking flower like gardenia and hibiscus which looks as though it ought only to be grown indoors. But this is far from the case, as they stand up well to the rigours of harsh winters. Camellias are happiest when grown in a sheltered position in lime-free soil where, on a frosty morning, they will not catch the rays of the early morning sun which could damage the flowers. They may be single, semi-double or double, in a wide range of shades from white to pink and red. Not only are their flowers beautiful but their all-the-year-round glossy green foliage is a joy to use, either fresh or glycerined. One of the most popular × *williamsii* varieties which can easily be obtained from most garden centres is 'Donation' with its semi-double silver pink blooms.

If you have large shrubs and don't mind cutting off sizeable branches, camellias make splendid pedestal arrangements. If, on the other hand, you only like to take a

14

few short stems with flowers and buds, they are ideal for table arrangements. They make a lovely centrepiece on a polished table sparkling with gleaming silver and shining crystal with linen napkins to match the colour of the flowers.

It is a natural step to move from thoughts of camellias, to magnolias. What a marvellous sight it is to see the lovely × *soulangiana* group with its white chalice-shaped flowers, stained rose-purple at the base against a pale blue sky. Although you need plenty of room for most magnolias there is one good species ideal for smaller gardens—M. Kobus var. *stellata*. It grows, very slowly, to a height of about ten feet with a similar spread. The lovely, star-shaped, white fragrant flowers appear in early spring, before the leaves open, and in full bloom it is a glorious sight. It lends itself well to Japanese-style arrangements when just a couple of carefully chosen small branches can make a breath-taking design.

Other shrubs which are suitable for the smaller garden are from the genus *Viburnum*. They are certainly shrubs for all seasons. In winter, some species flower on naked stems, in spring and summer others flower on leafy branches whilst some are grown mainly for their decorative fruits in autumn. Spring flowering kinds worth considering are × *carlcephalum* with rounded heads of sweetly scented pink and white flowers, and × *burkwoodii* with waxy,

fragrant, white flowers which are pink when in bud. Both these varieties blend beautifully in arrangements with the palest tulip varieties. Another eye-catcher in the garden is the *V. plicatum* 'Mariesii' with its many tiers of branches, weighed down with their white lace-cap-type flowers.

Spring is always associated with blossom and what a joy it is to arrange either in extravagant sweeping designs or in simple Japanese-inspired forms with just two or three branches. Cherry blossom is justly appreciated in Japan where the public go to enormous lengths, even staying away from work, to view the blossom and newspapers give the places and predicted days of the month for the best cherry blossom viewing!

The genus *Prunus* includes the most popular ornamentals, like almonds, peaches, plum, cherries and cherry laurels. In mid-spring *P. triloba* is a lovely sight with its bright green leaves and double rosette-like clear pink flowers.

The most popular cherry planted in gardens, where it often outgrows its position, is the bright pink 'Kanzan'. Sadly fewer people grow the 'Amanogawa' which with its columnar habit, grows high rather than wide. Arguably the most appealing cherry is white *P. avium* 'Plena' with its masses of double flowers, reminiscent of weddings when the blown petals cascade like confetti. The blossoming of white lilac, especially the *Syringa vulgaris* 'Vestale', is equally evocative. When using blossoms like lilac in an arrangement, it is a good idea to take off as many leaves as possible to make it last longer in water. One of the flower arranger's tricks is to remove all the leaves and introduce others on separate branches instead. Pear and apple blossom also are eye-catching features of the spring scene but should be left for fear of diminishing the fruit yield. However, if possible sneak a nicely shaped branch to use in a naturalistic arrangement with a group of bluebells—a combination which never fails to delight.

For the flower-arranger, spring brings forth two favourite plants, euphorbias and hostas. The perennial euphorbias range downwards from the giant-size *E. characias* and its subspecies *wulfenii* with a height and spread of about 120cm, 4ft and columnar panicles of yellow-green

flowers which are really bracts. The medium sized varieties such as *E. griffithii* with its flame-coloured bracts are about 60cm, 2ft in height and *E. amygdaloides var. robbiae* with pale green bracts grows to a similar size. A smaller type *E. polychroma* makes a brilliant splash of colour in the spring with its vivid yellow bracts. All these plants add a certain distinction to an arrangement because of their unusual form and colour. Great care should be taken when handling these flowers, once cut they exude a white sap which is highly irritant to sensitive skins. Do not on any account rub your eyes as it could be damaging. All such flower stems which bleed when cut should be held in a flame for a few seconds to seal the stem before giving them a long drink. The well-loved poinsettia which adds such striking colour to our Christmas arrangements is also a member of this genus.

Flower arrangers have done

a great deal to restore the popularity of many plants and this applies especially to the hosta. Each year the choice of new varieties gets larger and larger. They are superb plants to grow and create few problems except they are the favourite delicacy of the snail and slug population. They will grow in sun or shade. In a sunny position they tend to produce more of their trumpet-like flowers, whilst in the shade their leaves flourish on grander scale. Everyone's favourite must be the *H. fortunei* 'Albopicta'. In spring it is a splendid sight with its primrose yellow ovate leaves, edged with pale green, (they sadly lose their intense colour and revert to green as the season progresses). They add glamour to any arrangement and last well when cut as long as they are properly conditioned. For excellent results, float hostas over-night in a water-butt. Conveniently, hostas come in all sizes from the small, *H. undulata* with its wavy mid-green leaves splashed with white and silvery markings, to the giant-sized *H. sieboldiana* with its enormous glaucous corrugated leaves the size of rhubarb. In between the most popular are the medium-sized

H. crispula with prominent white margins and *H. fortunei* 'Aureomarginata' with yellow margins.

Another arresting spring foliage plant is *Iris pseudacorus* 'Variegata'. It is a true water iris and flourishes at the edge of a pool in shallow water; it will also grow in a water-retentive soil in the border although this will restrict its size. In early spring the leaves are predominantly bright yellow with green markings which fade as the season progresses. It is well worth cutting a few when they are at their most colourful stage and bringing them indoors to enjoy at close hand. Fortunately, this plant and the *Hosta fortunei* 'Albopicta' (already mentioned) are at their peak of perfection simultaneously and arranged together, with the addition of a few flowers, make a stunning sight.

Depending upon the size of your garden and whether you have a lime-free soil, rhododendrons and azaleas can be depended upon to give you lovely foliage as well as flowers. There are the smaller species of rhododendrons for the smaller garden as well as

the giants which can grow up to 12m, 40ft. The colours range from white, lemon, yellow and lavender to violet, pink, crimson, scarlet and orange. And the number of different species, varieties and hybrids runs into hundreds. So it is a case of going to a nursery or garden centre, paying your money and taking your choice.

These flowers are a delight to use in arrangements and they will last well if you first hammer or scrape the stems to enable them to take up a good supply of water before leaving them overnight in deep water. At the same time it is a good idea to remove a few leaves to show off the flowers better and to help make the flowers last longer. Rhododendrons make wonderful, dramatic arrangements on their own or they can be used to make an eye-catching focal point in mixed arrangements. Azaleas on the other hand, are much more fragile-looking and benefit from more delicate designs—that is, of course, if you can bring yourself to cut a few sprays of these slow-growing shrubs.

Although there is much to enjoy in the spring garden there is much to do as well. It is a good time to take stock of

your herbaceous border and decide if it can be improved in any way. Maybe a couple of plants could be transposed to give a better display or perhaps some of the older plants need dividing and replanting. Try to do this in spring rather than the autumn so that when they are replanted they have a better chance of more favourable weather.

This is also the time for sowing seed for some of your favourite bedding plants. Listed below are a few hardy (HA) and half-hardy annuals (HHA) which are well worth growing if you are interested in flower arranging. The hardy annuals can be sown in situ in early spring, but the half-hardy need to be sown under glass, hardened off and planted out later depending on local conditions.

AMARANTHUS CAUDATUS VAR. 'VIRIDIS' (HHA)
This is a green variety of the well-known 'love-lies-bleeding' which produces long trails up to 45cm, 18in long. Its unusual form adds interest to any arrangement.

ANTIRRHINUM (HHA)
There is a wide range to

Euphorbia Wulfenii

choose from both in form and colour. A recent addition is the Penstemon-flowered group which have an open, trumpet-like form such as 'Innovation mixed' which is excellent for cutting and gives much needed spikes for your arrangements.

ATRIPLEX HORTENSIS RUBRA (HA)

This plant has red foliage and red spikes of seeds in autuman and looks rather like the wild dock of the countryside. An unusual addition for your arranging.

CALENDULA (HA)

The somewhat disdained marigold is well worth growing especially 'Art Shades' a strain which includes bright and pastel colours. They look lovely in a cottage-style arrangement in a trug for example.

CLEOME SPINOSA (HHA)

An unusual plant not often seen in English gardens. It grows to about 1m, 3ft and is an erect plant with thorns at the base of the leaves. The flower heads are about 20cms, 4ins across made up of pink and white florets and always cause interest when used in an arrangement.

COBAEA SCANDENS (HHA)

A delightful quick climber which is often given the name 'cup and saucer' plant because of its unusual form. The flower is green when it opens and slowly changes to deep purple. There is a variety called 'Alba' which stays green throughout and is worth pursuing.

CUCURBITA (HHA)

These decorative gourds are fun to grow and use in your arrangements. They come in a wide variety from yellow and green striped to knobbly ones. They can either be displayed at the base of an arrangement or mounted on long wooden barbecue sticks to insert into your designs.

IPOMOEA (HHA)

Morning glories are grown in the garden more for the glorious sight they always make than for use in arrangements as they will only last a day. *I. tricolour* is a good one to try with its convolvulus flowers of bright blue in early morning fading to purple as the day wears on.

LARKSPUR (HA)

These are lovely annual delphiniums and well worth

growing for their tall spikes which are always useful to give height to your arrangements. They can have either single or double flowers and there is a choice of pink, purple or white.

MOLUCCELLA LAEVIS (HHA)

A must for all flower arrangers. The flowering spikes (up to 1m, 3ft) with branching stems are made up of small white flowers each surrounded by a pale green shell-like calyx. They look much more attractive in arrangements when the small white centre flower is taken out. They are spasmodic in germination but worth persevering with.

NICANDRA PHYSALOIDES (HHA)

Sometimes called the 'shoo-fly plant' as it is supposed to repel flies and is grown for the seed-heads rather than the flowers. The round fruits are enclosed by bright green and purple calyces.

NICOTIANA ALATA VAR. GRANDIFLORA (HHA).

The sweetly scented tobacco plant comes in a variety of colours—white, cream, pink,

crimson and yellow. But the one beloved by arrangers is 'Limelight', a marvellous acid green.

NIGELLA DAMASCENA (HA)

The common name is 'love-in-a-mist'. Pretty blue or white flowers are surrounded by feathery green tracery, but more noteworthy are their inflated fruit cases.

ORNAMENTAL KALE AND CABBAGES (HA)

These are unusual and fun to grow. The leaves are beautifully marked, either green and white or mauve and red. They are sometimes used as an unusual bedding display in parks and on traffic roundabouts.

PAPAVER (HA)

There are several varieties to choose from. The Iceland poppy, *P. nudicaule* is a delightful plant and comes in shades of red, apricot, white and cream. The Shirley poppy, *P. rhoeas* comes in shades of white, pink, rose, salmon and crimson. Another flower arranger's favourite is *P. somniferum* 'Pink Chiffon' with its full double pink flowers. All these flowers also provide the well-loved seedheads.

27

Cobaea Scandens

PETUNIAS (HHA)

The varieties fall into four main groups, multiflora, grandiflora, dwarf varieties and those with a long trailing habit which are ideal for urns and hanging baskets. The double 'Pan American All Double Mixed' with their large ruffled petals make excellent cut flowers.

RICINUS COMMUNIS SANGUINEUS (HHA)

The castor oil plant, which should not be confused with *Fatsia japonica*. It grows about 4ft, 120cm, high and has large bronze palmate leaves. The flowers are insignificant but the spiny seedheads are interesting. These dramatic leaves are excellent for foliage arrangements.

SALPIGLOSSIS (HHA)

This flower adds a real splash of colour to any garden with its velvety, veined petals which are multi-coloured in shades of crimson, scarlet, orange, yellow and lavender. Two worth trying are 'Grandiflora' and 'Splash'.

ZEA MAYS (HHA)

The maize variety *japonica variegata* produces beautiful green and cream striped leaves which should be fully mature when picked or they will flag. Their seed heads are also attractive to use.

ZINNIA ELEGANS

The dahlia-flowered strain are most popular with their fully double, flat-petalled flowers. If you want a mixture of colours—crimson, scarlet, lavender, violet, orange, yellow and white—try 'Giant Double Mixed'. But if you want something really special grow 'Envy', a wonderful lime-green flower which is superb.

Amaranthus

Summer

Summer is probably everyone's favourite season in the garden when even the gardener can find time to lie back with glass in hand and admire his or her handiwork. The perfect garden is not over tidy or regimented but rather a place of organized chaos where borders are chock-a-block with plants jostling each other for their place in the sun. Walls, trellis and posts are cascading with all kinds of delightful flowering climbers and trees and shrubs, which play host to others, are festooned with canopies of bloom. Tubs, urns and chimney pots like giant cornucopiae overflow with their own particular treasure, adding a final flourish to the burgeoning scene. Every year the sheer extravagance of it all is overpowering but stop admiring for a moment to make a mental note of alterations where plant associations can be improved or where highlights can be added to a rather dull area.

Whilst spring is a time of expectation, summer is the realization. Slowly and imperceptibly the border fills out and the bare earth is hidden once more. The skyline alters as the trees come into full leaf and the garden has that satisfying enclosed feeling

again. The days lengthen and it is worth developing a ritual to walk in the garden after breakfast when everything looks pristine and again in the late evening when the garden is rich with the fragrance of the flowers. In the heat of high noon, set aside the garden tools and indulge in an *al fresco* lunch taken beneath a giant garden umbrella.

Early summer is normally associated with roses and they must surely be the most popular flower with two thousand different types now available from nurseries and garden centres. The Royal National Rose Society's Gardens of the Rose at St Albans in Hertfordshire grows some thirty thousand specimens representing over a thousand varieties. There are roses for every situation, from the miniatures growing no more than 20–30cm, 8–12in, ideal for growing in urns and window boxes, to the vigorous giants which can climb 9–12m, 30–40ft to embellish an old tree. In between there are hybrid teas (now classed as large flowered) and floribunda (cluster flowered) along with the tall-stemmed standards and for those with plenty of space, the shrub roses, which always delight with their exuberance of fragrant blooms. Colour is very personal and to recommend particular roses might not satisfy all tastes. The best way to make your own selection would be to visit a rose nursery when they are in full bloom.

Roses with their infinite variety of colour and form are one of the flower arranger's favourite flowers. They need little embellishment and look delightful when arranged *en masse* or in two's and three's with their own foliage. Large flowered roses make excellent centres of interest for more flamboyant pedestal designs, while fragrant blooms are especially delightful for dinner table designs when arranged in low crystal or silver containers. Here are a few of the floribundas which are particularly useful in arrangements—'Elizabeth of Glamis' (apricot), 'Iceberg' (white), 'Dearest' (soft pink), 'Iced Ginger' (ivory and copper) and 'The Flower Arranger' (pearly peach). Excellent hybrid teas include—'Whisky Mac' (deep amber), 'Doris Tysterman' (tangerine orange with bronze foliage), 'Peace' (lemon edged with pink), 'Fragrant Cloud' (dusty red with a wonderful perfume) and the superb 'Silver Jubilee' (pink, apricot and cream). This last is a must for any garden, the perfect blooms of this exquisite rose cannot fail to please. Two old shrub roses worth a mention are 'Fantin-Latour' (pale pink) and 'Mme Isaac Pereire' (deep pink) possibly the most fragrant of all these roses. A modern shrub rose which is incomparable, provided you have room, is named after the inspirational flower arranger Constance Spry. It has large delicate pink blooms with deeper pink centres and a sweet perfume.

There is always space in any garden for a climbing rose whether for a wall, a trellis, a fence or a post. Two good examples are 'Golden Showers' (gold-yellow) and 'Handel' (cream and pink). Another is the well-loved thornless Bourbon climber 'Zephirine Drouhin' with its semi-double scented carmine flowers but it is prone to mildew and black spot. Such blights make regular spraying necessary but it is a small price to pay for the unending pleasure healthy and luxuriant roses give us all summer long.

Grow 'Zephirine Drouhin' on a trellis near large-flowered clear blue *Clematis* 'Lasurstern' so the blooms intermingle to make a breathtaking sight.

The large flowering *Clematis*

look so fragile yet they are perfectly hardy and most accommodating. As well as growing them against walls and through host plants, they can be grown in containers for those with small patio gardens. Suitable *Clematis* for container growing are 'Comtesse de Bouchaud' (mauve pink), 'Perle d'Azur' (deep blue) and 'Madame Edouard Andre' (dusky red). As well as the floriferous *C. montana* try 'Hagley Hybrid' (rosy mauve), 'Miss Bateman' (creamy white) and the ever-popular old timer 'Nelly Moser' (mauve pink with a lilac bar). Two gorgeous doubles worth seeking out are 'Vyvyan Pennell' (lavender) and

'Duchess of Edinburgh' (white with green outer sepals) as well as 'Edith' (white). These lovely, delicate-looking flowers can be used in arrangements if you lightly crush and singe the cut stem before plunging into deep water for several hours. They look delightfully exotic when added to large extravagant 'Dutch' arrangements or used in a dinner table design.

For a novel and captivating centrepiece take a silver dish and pile upon it a few bunches of green and purple grapes which have been frosted and among them tuck in a few mauve clematis and ivy trails. These can be inserted in small orchid tubes

Passion Flower

egg-white, liberally dredge them with castor sugar and leave them to dry in a warm place. Instead of *Clematis* apply the same idea with fleeting yet fascinating passion flowers.

Many people only know of the passion flower (*Passiflora caerulea*) as a greenhouse plant where its size is often restricted. The name derives from the fact that the component parts of this intriguing flower are symbolic of Christ's crucifixion. Grown outdoors on a south facing trellis it can reach splendid proportions with masses of flowers which occasionally produce oval yellow fruits.

Honeysuckle is another favourite climbing plant which, like *Clematis*, prefers to have its head in the sun and its feet in the shade. One lovely hybrid is *Lonicera × tellmanniana* with bright yellow tubular flowers tipped with bronze, but sadly it has no scent. For those who must have perfume there are the

which are easy to secrete among the grapes. Frosted fruits are always delightful to use in many ways and so easy to prepare. Just paint over your chosen fruits with beaten

36

early Dutch forms to choose from and they will usually put on a second display of blossom towards the summer's end.

The scents of the flowers add an important dimension to any garden and for this purpose the lily family take some beating. *Lilium regale* with its heady perfume and perfect flowers with glistening white petals suffused with gold at the centre and flushed with rose-pink on the reverse is a splendid plant. As you can see from any bulb catalogue the choice of lilies is now enormous with hybrids in shades of lime–yellow, gold, pale orange, apricot, pink and mauve. It is fun to try a few new ones each year as others become victims of the dreaded virus disease. If you want to have something really remarkable try *L. auratum* with its beautifully marked, spectacularly large flowers. They can be grown outside or in pots in the greenhouse as can *L. longiflorum* (Easter lily). Possibly the best known lily of all is *L. candidum* (Madonna lily) a species which has been cultivated for over three thousand years and which we always associate with old cottage gardens. Two other outdoor flowering lilies, each with Turk's cap flowers, are *L.*

martagon which thrives well in semi-woodland conditions and the *L. lancifolium tigrinum* (tiger lily). Have a large brilliant orange splash of these to emblazen the border. They can be grown from the tiny bulbils which form in the leaf axils and within three years will reach their magnificent best.

Other flower arranging 'freebies' which seed themselves in some of the most unlikely yet inspired places are *Alchemilla mollis* and *Tellima grandiflora*. Both have tiny flowers of lime-green and always add an extra sparkle to any arrangement. There is something about greenish coloured flowers that excites most arrangers, and for this reason eucomis never fails to surprise and delight. It is an unusual flower, resembling a green pineapple on a stick. Its tiny star-shaped green flowers, which are clustered around and up the stem, are edged with maroon and it has a tuft of pale green leaves at the top. Another curious flower rescued from obscurity by arrangers is astrantia. It has star-like greenish-pink flowers bordered with a frill of bracts of the same colour tipped with green. There is an all-pink variety *A. Carniolica Rubra* and another with beautifully marked variegated leaves.

Early summer is the time for peonies when their voluminous heads like giant cabbage roses can be seen swaggering in the border. A lovely one to grow is 'Bowl of Beauty', it has semi-double soft pink flowers with conspicuous golden stamens. The peonies are wonderful flowers for using on the grand scale and look superb with some of the tall spikes from the herbaceous border, chosen from flowers like the delphiniums, *Digitalis* (foxglove) especially the Excelsior hybrids, *aruncus* (Goat's beard), *angelica*, *campanula* and lupins. The hollow-stemmed flowers such as *angelica* and lupins will last quite well when cut if you fill up their stems with water and plug the ends with cotton wool before giving them a long drink.

Although the bearded iris, those wonderful flowers with their spectacular markings, are over by summer there are others of the same family to enjoy. Particularly lovely is the *I. ochroleuca* (now correctly *I. orientalis*) with its slightly twisted 1m, 3ft leaves and its succession of large white flowers with blotches of

38

Lilium Candidium

yellow. The *I. sibiricas* is much daintier, with smaller flowers borne high above the foliage on tall stems which appear in several shades of pale blue, dark blue and white. And a real eye-opener is the *I. kaempferi* with 'Higo' as a good strain producing flowers some 20cm, 8 in across which look like giant butterflies.

A well-planted herbaceous border provides interest all summer long and as one plant matures and fades, so another takes over like waves on the shore. Those giant back-of-the-border flowers—the *inula*, Mullein (Verbascum) and *Macleaya* appear later in a wave of colour. Inula has leaves the size of dinner plates and unusual daisy-like flowers with fine twisted yellow petals while the *Verbascum* has tall spikes of yellow flowers and grey-green woolly-haired leaves. The *Macleaya*, known also as *Bocconia* or plume poppy, is perhaps less well known. It produces tall spires of buff-coloured, feathery flowers with large deeply-lobed leaves which are bronze above and grey beneath. Be careful when you handle them as they exude a bright yellow dye when cut, as a precaution, seal them in a flame. In stunning

contrast, have a mass of orange Alstroemerias which is despised by many as being an invasive plant but revels in bright shining flowers. Later it produces useful and interesting inflated seedheads which you can hear popping as they dry off. Nearby in the border plant Crocosmia, a genus which now contains the former Montbretia and *Curtonus*, all members of the Iris family. With pleated mid-green leaves they make good bed-fellows for the *Kniphofia* (red-hot poker). Less flamboyant are the more subtly coloured hybrids like 'Bee's Lemon' (rich lemon-yellow), 'Bee's Sunset' (flame orange) and 'Maid of Orleans' (ivory cream). Other smaller plants, not to be overlooked because they are so interesting, are *Sisyrinchium striatum* and *Liatris* (Kamas Gay Feather). The former has star-shaped, cream-yellow flowers clustered up its stem with iris-type leaves. It is possible to find a variegated form with attractive green and cream markings on the leaves. The *Liatris* is unusual, perverse even, because its purple spikes start flowering at the top and work downwards whilst most flowers do the opposite.

Another unusual plant to be coveted, until you acquire your own, is *Veratrum album*. This fascinating plant has accordion-pleated leaves which ascend the stem until they reach its plume-shaped flowering head which consists of tiny greenish-white flowers. So arresting is this plant, you will find yourself visiting and revisiting it to ensure it is

Crocosmia Masonorum

quite real.

Lilies have already been mentioned but not to be excluded are *Hemerocallis* (day-lilies) which brighten up the border for weeks on end. Although each flower lasts only for a day, the numerous buds to each flowering stem open in turn to give a long succession of bloom. There are many to choose from in shades of yellow, apricot, bronze-red, pink and mauve. Another hardy perennial which adds great pools of colour to the border is the Phlox with its sumptuous round heads in shades of pink, mauve, purple, and red; some are self-coloured while others have bright centres. The white Phlox have a brilliance which would be a good advertisement for any soap powder!

This is a wonderful time of the year if you are called upon to do wedding arrangements for the church and the home as there is such an abundance of choice. Great branches of *Philadelphus* with orange-blossom scented flowers make ideal outlines coupled with sprays of Whitebeam displayed in reverse showing the silver backs of their leaves. Masses of lovely white flowers such as

41

Delphiniums, foxgloves, Astilbes, *Lysimachia clethroides*, lilies, roses, peonies, Phlox, Gladioli and *Galtonia candicans* along with silvery-grey artichoke leaves make elegant pedestal designs. The addition of frothy lime-green flowers from *Alchemilla mollis* with dainty heads of fennel or cow parsley can work wonders and give formal designs a certain lightness of touch. Smaller arrangements for the home can be made with marguerites, sweet peas, Aquilegias, pinks, carnations, roses and Nigella. Make use of any of the more dainty flowers you might have blooming in the garden which would give the desired ethereal touch ideal for such an occasion.

Summer weddings promote thoughts of summer entertaining, and it is a great asset to have the garden as an extra 'room' provided, of course, the sun is smiling. There is something special about entertaining *al fresco*, it seems so much more carefree and informal and the hostess can be carefree of anything spilt on the ground. Barbecues are a marvellous idea, and if you have a special paved area for such occasions, it is fun to embellish it with groups of colourful pot plants from the

greenhouse as well as doing the flowers. If you prefer something a little grander build a raised-up arrangement of fruits and flowers, they add an extra sparkle to an atmosphere already heightened by food and wine. But for a luncheon party a smaller central arrangement would be more appropriate with flowers selected to enhance the colours already chosen for the linen and china.

Flowers and plants grown in containers have numerous uses in the garden. They can accentuate a special feature or enhance a view, they can conceal a problem area or give prominence to a specially cherished plant. It is a case of choosing the right container for the right position. Tubs, pots, urns, sinks and even chimney pots, especially those from period houses, all make wonderful containers. The most colourful and accommodating plants for these situations are the popular ones, probably because they cannot be beaten. For height I like the variously coloured fuchsias along with pelargoniums (geraniums), petunias and tuberous begonias (which should be started off in the greenhouse and planted out when there is no fear of frost). Enchanting pale and dark blue trailing lobelia spills in profusion down the sides of the containers, and as with hanging baskets there should, be a mass of luxuriant bloom for great effect. Foliage plants can also look spectacular grown this way. There are some beautifully marked *Phormium* (New Zealand flax) now available with pink and maroon leaves and an appropriately named one called 'Cream Delight'. These are not as hardy as the more popular 'Variegatum' and 'Purpureum' and it is an excellent idea to grow them in containers when they can be over-wintered indoors. Hostas grown this way are free from the ravages of the slug and snail population which can turn a leaf into something resembling lace in an astonishingly short space of time. The ideal pest control is achieved with the presence of a hedgehog but sadly these delightful creatures are not always to order.

Ferns are not everyone's favourite plant except perhaps the *Nephrolepsis* which seems to be the number one in the house plant stakes. But there are some striking hardy ones

well worth seeking out from specialist nurseries. There is one with delicate pink, mauve and grey fronds known as the Japanese painted fern which is much easier to remember than *Athyrium nipponicum goeringianum pictum*. A handsome fern which thrives best in moist conditions is the *Osmunda regalis* (royal fern) which usually grows to a height of 1.30m, 4ft although it is said to attain a height of 3m, 10ft in the wild! Another difficult name to remember, and even harder to pronounce, is the *Polystichum setiferum plumoso-divisilobum* but it is surely the king of the outdoor ferns. It has fronds which are finely divided and overlap, presenting a mass of beautiful greenery to marvel at. These outstanding ferns will last well

in your arrangements but do remember to cut only the mature ones otherwise they will flop at the tips and spoil your design.

Many gardeners have very definite views about dahlias—they either love them or hate them. They are wonderful cut-and-come-again flowers with a never-ending succession of blooms which present a kaleidoscope of colour from mid-spring until they are cut down by the first autumn frosts. They look better grown in a bed of their own and are easier to manage this way with the replanting and lifting of their tubers each year. If you have a light, well-drained soil you can often get away with leaving them in the ground as long as you give

the bed extra protection in the winter. Dahlias come in all shapes and sizes—there are huge giant decoratives (beloved by the show fraternity) and tiny pompoms, as well as the single, anemone and peony-flowered, the cactus and the collarette and others to choose from in every colour of the rainbow except blue. Try building up a dahlia bed with a collection of pompoms, medium decoratives and cactus which fall within four main colour schemes. For example choose dahlias in a variety of lemon, pink and mauve, adding a few red ones for the dramatic effect they have in modern flower arrangements. Such organization is recommended as with impulsively bought tubers you can end up with an unhappy hotch-potch of colour.

Even though summer allows you to snatch a couple of hours every now and then to laze in the garden, thoughts of outstanding chores insidiously intrude. Your peaceful reverie is disturbed and you are on the move again. There are hedges to be trimmed, grass to be seen to, beds to be weeded, plants to be staked, pruning to be done, and plants to be sprayed, paths to be tended, patios to be swept, dead-heading to be done, plants to be fed—all jobs which any gardeners worth their salt take in their stride and, believe it or not, really enjoy!

Autumn

In some ways autumn seems rather a sad season of the year, bringing to an end the cycle of yet another year's growth in the garden; nevertheless it has its compensations. Each year one cannot fail to wonder at the sheer beauty and brilliance of the autumn foliage when illuminated by the low rays of the season's gentle sunlight. Who has not found delight in the sight of cobwebs shimmering with dewdrops as they festoon the trees and shrubs on misty mornings or indulged in the evocative smell of distant bonfires while kicking through brittle fallen leaves? Who has not marvelled at the fruit trees bowed down with their autumn bounty, and noticed the berries on trees and shrubs awaiting plunder by the hungry birds? There is no cause for melancholy. It is harvest-time for all of us—the gardener, the flower arranger, the birds and beasts.

Even though many flowers in the garden are past their best there are still some which will carry on flowering—roses, clematis, dahlias and chrysanthemums as well as the

latecomers in the herbaceous border. Some of these later flowering varieties which I like to use in arrangements come within a yellow and brown colour scheme. The sometimes despised *Solidago* (golden rod) which grows to a height of about 2m, 6ft, is most useful for defining the outlines of large designs. If you prefer something smaller the hybrids 'Goldenmosa' (yellow) and 'Lemore' (primrose yellow) grow only to a height of 60cm,

2ft. Two highly recommended achilleas are 'Coronation Gold' and 'Gold Plate'—both have large flat heads of deep yellow but for those who like a paler yellow, 'Moonshine' is the one to grow. *Rudbeckias*, always useful at this time of the year, with varieties of *R. fulgida* such as 'Deamii' and 'Goldsturm', have large bright yellow flowers with dark brown centres. Another member of this family is the 'Gloriosa' daisy, (including

singles, doubles and *R. nitida* 'Herbstsonne') which is also known as the coneflower. Finally I must mention the *Helenium autumnale*, which has many-headed free flowering daisy-like flowers with prominent domed brown centres. Others worth considering are 'Butterpat' (rich yellow), 'Latest Red' (rich bronze red) and 'Mahogany' (red and golden brown). All these flowers look delightful when arranged together against a background of colourful foliage which, according to taste, either matches or contrasts. If you want to further intensify the colour scheme, try introducing long branches of golden privet together with some larger yellow-flecked leaves of the spotted laurel (*Aucuba*). Many people only think of privet as hedging material; as such it is trimmed out of all recognition, but it would grow into a splendid tree if given the chance. If, on the other hand, you would like a contrast to this vivid yellow colour scheme, a background of glycerined beech would be an alternative.

Another popular colour scheme for autumn flowers from the herbaceous border falls within the deep pink,

Eryngium Alpinum

dark red and purple range. For this you can have the *Aster* (michaelmas daisy), *Anemone japonica*, *Eryngium*, *Eupatorium*, *Lavandula* (lavender), *Monarda*, *Penstemon*, *Salvia*, *Sedum* and *Verbena*. For those who are not *au fait* with *Eryngium* (the sea holly belongs to this genus) there are two or three treasures I should like to recommend. The flowers of this unusual plant resemble small teasel heads which are surrounded with a collar of spiked bracts and their bluish purple metallic sheen makes them an unusual addition to any border or flower arrangement. *E. Alpinum* is a splendid specimen. It is about 60cm, 2 ft high and has a marvellous tracery of spiny bracts resembling the extravagant lace collars worn by the Cavaliers. The hybrid *E. × oliverianium* has equally large flower heads and the *E. tripartitum* has much smaller flowers but more of them. The *Sedum* is represented in many gardens by the aptly named hybrid 'Autumn Joy'. It gives three bites of the cherry—use it in the green stage, again when it is colouring up and finally when it matures into its deep burgundy red. It is beloved by bees, moths and butterflies and takes over from

the *Buddleia davidii* (commonly known as the butterfly bush) when it dies back. With the rich range of colours from this array of flowers the choice of equally rich coloured foliage would add to the splendour of your arrangements and two immediately spring to mind. The metallic blue-grey of the *Eucalyptus gunnii* which will grow quickly in the garden provided it is planted in a sheltered spot and the *Rosa rubrifolia*. This splendid rose will grow quickly to a height of 2m, 7 ft in spite of constant cutting and you will find its purple stems with leaves of blue-grey a constant joy to use. In autumn the leaves are splashed with yellow and purple and the masses of rich red hips make it a wonderful sight.

Metal containers seem to have an affinity with autumn colour schemes. In this case pewter would be ideal, so choose something like a large plate or platter, or a larger tankard or pitcher to hold your flowers.

Pewter, too, is a marvellous foil for *Hydrangea* flowers which colour up so beautifully at this time of the year. It is justifiably one of our most popular shrubs. The ones we see most often are from the

species *H. macrophylla* and there are many named varieties from which to choose. These are divided into two groups, the Hortensia with their large mop-heads and the Lacecaps with their flat heads. Both come in a variety of colours from brilliant blue to deep pink. However, the type of soil in which they grow, whether alkaline or acid, can influence their colour. As they turn colour cut these flowers for drying but wait until they have a papery feel before doing so. Stand them where it is warm in a jar holding about an inch of water and allow them gradually to dry off. In this way they often retain their autumnal colouration and make wonderful centres

of interest in large dried arrangements. The same method of drying should also be used for achillea.

There are many other flowers in the garden which lend themselves to drying but success depends on picking them at just the right time. The *Acanthus mollis* sometimes known as bear's breeches, with its 1m, 3ft long spires of white and purple flowers should be cut when the florets are open right to the top. No arranger should be without *Alchemilla mollis* (lady's mantle) and although it is mostly used when it is a frothy mass of tiny lime-green flowers, it can also be dried and does retain a good colour. The long green and maroon tassels of

Amaranthus caudatus (love-lies-bleeding) are well worth drying because of the unusual form of the flowers which always add interest to any arrangement. The *Physalis alkekengii* (Chinese lanterns) should be cut as soon as they have turned orange although sometimes you can use them in arrangements when they are still in their green stage. A majestic plant for the back of the border and one which produces wonderful flower heads for drying, is *Cynara cardunculus* (cardoon). A close relative and equally useful is the *C. scolymus* (globe artichoke). Earlier in the year these plants produce splendid 1m, 3ft long serrated grey leaves which are ideal for those giant arrangements which are often called for at church festivals. Some other flowers worth monitoring for cutting are *Echinops* (globe thistle) and *Eryngium*, three types of which I have already recommended to grow in the border. Flowers such as *Anaphalis*, as well as the true everlasting ones like the *Helichrysum*, especially grown for drying, should be examined regularly so that they can be cut at just the right time. All these flowers should be dried off in a warm situation, hanging them upside down so that the tops of their stems are left rigid. An old clothes rack stood on its side makes an excellent drying frame for this purpose.

As well as harvesting your flowers it is an excellent time, too, for collecting seedheads before they disintegrate or get eaten by the birds. The wonderful *Allium* (onion) group provide many favourites especially *A. albopilosum* with its great round 25cms, 10in, starburst seedheads. If you agree that big is beautiful other large seedheads which are superb to use in large modern designs are from the *Angelica* and the giant hog-weed. Both make bold exclamation marks in any border as well as evoking marked exclamations from non-gardening friends. Another giant plant, this time with smaller seedheads, is *Dipsacus fullonum* (teasel) an incomparable plant. Not only does it give flowers and seedheads but keeps you well supplied with false stems for many other uses. Like the *Angelica* it is a biennial and when they are reaching maturity they both die off. However, once you have them you will never be without a constant supply as they are self-seeding and give a mass of little plants to pass on to other flower arranging friends. It is the right time, too, to collect

Typha latifolia (reedmace) which is incorrectly called the bulrush by many people. There is a small species *T. minima* often grown in garden ponds but if this is not available, it is worth taking a trip into the nearby countryside to collect a few from the edge of a pond or stream and at the same time keep an eye open for some dead stalks of wild dock, both of which will give you much needed height in your dried arrangements. There are also one or two 'dwarfs' which dry beautifully—like the inflated seedheads of *Nigella* (love-in-a-mist) and the fluffy heads of various varieties of *Clematis* especially *C. tangutica*. Two types of unusual tiered seedheads to dry are from the candelabra group of *Primula* and from *Phlomis russeliana*, an interesting plant which in summer produces three or four whorls of yellow flowers borne at intervals up their stems. And perhaps the widest known of all dried seedheads is *Lunaria* (honesty) with its distinctive silver discs. When first picked these are not apparent as the translucent membrane, upon which the seeds sit, is covered with another tougher skin which is easily removed by tweaking between the finger and thumb when they are completely dry. Sometimes they can be equally effective when used in their green and purple stages, before they finally dry off.

Two other seedheads which give a splash of colour to the autumn garden are from the *Phytolacca americana* (poke weed) and the *Iris foetidissima* (stinking iris). The poke weed is an unusual plant, rarely grown in the garden but nevertheless it is prized by arrangers. It grows to a height of 120–150cm, 4–5ft and bears 15cm, 6 in spikes of tiny star-shaped green flowers which gradually change to green fruits. As they mature these fruits look for all the world like blackberries clustered together on a stem. They should be handled with care as not only are the roots and berries poisonous but the berries will stain anything they touch. On second thoughts,

maybe this is why they are not very popular! The 'stinking' iris is so cruelly named because of the rank smell it allegedly gives off when the leaves are bruised. Its dark green, evergreen leaves are especially valuable in the winter time. It produces rather dingy flowers which present no temptation to the arranger. This is fortunate as uncut they are able to form their wonderful seedheads which burst open in the autumn to reveal rows of striking orange berries. Fortunately these seeds do not immediately fall out of their pods when they open but remain intact for quite a while. Another advantage of this plant is that it thrives in the shade.

It is the brilliance and the bounty of the berries in the autumn garden which excite, although they are there only for a short time. The sight of a group of *Sorbus* (rowan)

flowering Crab Apples

trees, each a mass of colourful berries some red, others orange or pink and even white with their leaves splashed with their fiery autumn tints cannot fail to stop people in their tracks in sheer wonderment. But for those who do not have space for such plantings there is a wide variety of smaller trees and shrubs which will produce a kaleidoscope of

60

coloured berries—for you as well as the birds! It is worth remembering when you are making your choice, that the birds will go for the orange and red berries first and that they tend to ignore the yellow and white ones. Among the most popular trees and shrubs which produce colourful fruits are *Berberis*, *Cotoneaster*, *Ilex* (holly), *Lonicera* (honeysuckle), *Malus* (crab apple), *Pernettya*, *Pyracantha* (firethorn), *Rosa rugosa* and *R. moyesii*, *Skimmia*, *Symphoricarpos* (snowberry) and *Viburnum opulus* (guelder rose).

Whilst these branches covered with berries will always give a certain panache to any arrangement, they can look delightful used another way. Make a cone or pyramid arrangement by inserting short-stemmed flowers and leaves into a conically shaped piece of floral foam standing on some kind of compote. Tiny groups of berries can be added as a final flourish where they will shine like jewels in a richly encrusted ornament. A couple of these matching designs would be ideal for decorating a buffet table.

Perhaps the most breath-taking sight of all in any garden at this time of the year is the trees and shrubs whose foliage blaze away like a giant bonfire before they finally shed their leaves. Trees like *Acer japonicum* (maple) which turns a rich crimson and *A. tataricum* a golden yellow; *Liquidambar* whose five-pointed green leaves turn brilliant orange and scarlet; *Parrotia persica* with amber, crimson and gold foliage and *Quercus borealis* (red oak) which turns from a dull crimson to deep red brown and a near relative *Q. coccinea*, which in its turn changes to scarlet. There are also some shrubs which dress themselves up in flamboyant colours for their last performance of the year. Shrubs like the *Azaleas* many of whose Ghent hybrids exhibit their richly coloured autumn foliage; *Cornus florida* (dogwood) whose green leaves are splashed with yellow, bronze and red; *Cotinus coggygria* (smoke bush) which takes on a brilliant orange colour while 'Atropurpureus' (the purple variety) takes on light red tints; *Enkianthus cernuus* whose green leaves assume orange and red tints; *Fothergilla major* showing off its array of orange, red and yellow colours; *Hamamelis × intermedia* 'Jelena' ablaze with leaves which have turned to orange, bronze and red; *Mahonia bealei* which

sometimes has leaves which have turned brilliant red and *Rhus typhina* (stag's horn sumach) a shrub often seen in front gardens with its striking orange-red, yellow and purple foliage. And talking of brilliant foliage, *Parthenocissus* (Virginia creeper) cannot be omitted. One of the most popular creepers, at this time of the year it can make a ramshackle house look like a most desirable residence.

Even amidst all this autumn colour there are still a few flowering trees and shrubs to admire like the *Eucryphia*

× *nymansensis*, an evergreen hybrid which in autumn is a mass of delicate single four petalled rose-like flowers and the *Clerodendron*. Two species worth mentioning are *C. bungei* which has flattened terminal heads of fragrant rose-pink flowers and *C. thomsonae*, an evergreen climber which produces 15cm, 6in pendular panicles of lantern-shaped cream and red flowers. And just when you think the lily-like *Crinum* × *powellii* will not be flowering this year, its sturdy stems with many flowering buds suddenly appear from a mass of long straggly leaves. The lovely blue *Agapanthus* continues to flower during autumn so place nearby a patch of the most brilliant blue one can imagine—*Gentiana sino-ornata*. The showy colchicums (autumn crocus) which always look a bit lost without any leaves, are also in flower. Possibly the last bulbous plant to flower in the garden is the *Nerine bowdenii* and the sight of a group of its brilliant pink heads in the late autumn is certainly a tonic to a jaded gardener.

Even in autumn there is still work to do in the garden; it is after all the beginning of the spring bulb planting time. Bulbs of the *Narcissus* family should be planted as early as possible, (already mentioned in the spring section of this book) as well as some of the other delightful small spring flowers like the *Crocus*, *Chionodoxa*, *Muscari* and *Scilla*. The hyacinths, too, should be planted when you have cleared away your summer bedding plants but the tulips

Gentiana Sino-Ornata

are best planted in late autumn as earlier planting may expose the early growth to frost damage.

Now is also the time for planting trees and shrubs, as well as taking hardwood cuttings to increase some of your favourites already in the garden and don't forget the shrub roses and the more vigorous cluster-flowering roses at the same time. Some hardy annuals like larkspur, marigolds and cornflowers can be sown outdoor for earlier flowering. Lift the tuberous begonias as well as the gladioli which have given you a splendid display all summer and dry them off for next year. Take in any geraniums and fuchsias you wish to over-winter indoors. The dahlias, too, have to be lifted, dried off and stored after they are cut down by the first frost.

A gardener's work, like a woman's, is never done and other jobs remain like sweeping up the leaves from the lawn and ensuring the garden pond is covered with some form of mesh to keep out the fallen leaves which can pollute the water and sometimes kill the fish. Tidy up the garden generally in autumn so that there are not too many places for pests to spend the winter. Finally, take steps to protect tender treasures from the ravages of the winter to come. Lay died-off leaves and stems over them like an eiderdown, so that when spring comes you can look forward to their happy return.

Winter

Winter strips away the final flourish of autumn's carnival and we are left again with the stark reality of the garden in its skeletal form. The silhouettes of the deciduous trees and shrubs are etched against the sky while the conifers stand like sentinels in their alloted places and the earth is bare once more. The skyline opens again and views, lost when the garden was clad in all its finery, reappear as if by magic. The fleeting sunshine lights up the remaining berries on the shrubs where they glisten like bright jewels and the rain makes the leaves of the evergreens shine like patent leather. A walk round the garden after a hoar frost has its pleasures—rimy seedheads, shrubs and cobwebs shimmer in the greyish light. Even the snowy weather has its compensations. Most people still secretly get the same thrill as they did as children when throwing back the curtains on a winter's morning to find the garden transformed into a glistening scene of breath-taking splendour.

Now is the time to appreciate the quieter beauty of many of the trees and shrubs which during the summer and autumn months are overpowered by their more flamboyant neighbours. And where would we be without the conifers which are so important in establishing a permanent frame-work for any garden? They give shelter and solidity as well as all-the-year–round interest. They come in a wide variety of foliage textures and colours and do best in damp and slightly acid soils, although some species can be grown in chalk and limestone conditions. This genera includes giants like the *Sequoia sempervirens* (coast redwood)—the tallest recorded tree of this species well over three hundred feet in height is rather too large for the average garden, down to the more amenable dwarf forms ideally suited to rock and scree gardens. Well worth mentioning are the wonderful range of yellow foliaged conifers which need to be planted in full sun to preserve their bright colour. One suitable for the smaller garden is *Chamaecyparis lawsoniana* 'Ellwood's Gold'. It is a slow-growing compact columnar variety reaching a height of 2m, 6ft. A taller well-recommended species growing to about 5m, 15ft is the *C. obtusa* 'Crippsii'. Another popular yellow conifer, but this time for the rockery or heather bed is *Thuja occidentalis* 'Rheingold'. All these colourful shrubs make a wonderful sight when they are lit up by the winter sunshine.

Colourful foliage like this is a godsend to arrangers throughout the winter months and singled out for special mention is the splendid golden yew *Taxus baccata* 'Elegantissima'. To ring the changes arrangers delight in using a few small branches of the blue-grey *Cedrus atlantica* 'Glauca' and *Chamaecyparis lawsoniana* 'Pembury Blue'. One conifer which is freely available from most florists' shops is *Tsuga heterophylla* (western hemlock) and it is worth growing in the garden if space is available. It is a great favourite of arrangers as its delicate flowing branches make wonderful outlines for both large and small arrangements. Curiously, it is seen at its best if you reverse the branches to show off the lovely glaucous backing of the leaves.

Space does not permit me to write more about conifers and though I have only mentioned

a few yellow and glaucous varieties the overall choice is infinite. Nevertheless, it needs care to make sure you have selected the right kind of plant for the right place.

Conifers have their place in heath and heather gardens too, but they must be carefully selected so that they do not grow out of scale in the overall scheme of things. Such

gardens can provide colour all the year round if they are astutely planted and there are some superb examples. The heathers remain in bloom for many weeks, sometimes even months, and they are largely free from pests and diseases except maybe honey fungus. Recommended winter flowering kinds of *Erica carnea* are 'Praecox Rubra' (deep rich pink), 'Snow Queen' (white), 'King George' (rose pink) and two hybrids *E. × darleyensis* 'Darley Dale' (pale purple pink) and

'Silberschmelze' (white).

Somehow I never think of conifers without thinking of Christmas. They are as much a part of festive decorations as the holly and the ivy. If you are fortunate enough to have a fruiting holly tree in the garden, it is a good idea to cover some of the berried branches with netting early in the winter. You may rob the birds of part of their festive feast but you will have some left for your decorations.

At Christmas I love to see holly wreaths festooned with

bright red ribbon fastened to the front door, trails of evergreens above the fireplace and evergreen swags looped up the staircase with ribbon bows. Christmas arrangements are fun to do and add so much to the festivities by their sheer exuberance. Even if you are pressed for time at this busy season, arrangements of greenery can be made early and left in a sheltered spot in the garden where they can be kept well watered. When they are required you can bring them indoors and titivate them by adding a few fresh flowers like red carnations, white chrysanthemums or even the wonderfully colourful poinsettias.

Favourite hollies are the variegated forms and if you want berries you must be sure to grow both female and male plants. *Ilex* × *altaclarensis* 'Golden King' is, despite its name, the female of the species with golden margined leaves and large red berries and *I. aquifolium* 'Golden Queen', also with gold margined leaves, is the male form. Alternatively there are hollies with silver-edged leaves and you can obtain both male and female plants of *I. a.* 'Argentei-marginata'.

I am often astounded at some people's hostility towards ivy, they won't even consider having it in the garden as they say it will either kill their trees or pull down their walls. To be influenced by such old wives' tales means that they deprive themselves of growing this excellent plant. Ivy has two forms of growth, the runner growth with lobed leaves and aerial roots for clinging to surfaces, and the aborescent growth with wavy margined leaves, but without aerial roots. This growth is produced when the runner growth reaches the top of its own particular means of support. Incidentally, cuttings taken from this arborescent growth will develop into bushy flowering and fruiting shrubs known as tree ivies. Climb ivy up walls, along fences or round posts—it is a marvellous way to display ivy and the more rampant varieties are easier to keep in check this way. *Hedera canariensis* 'Gloire de Marengo' is familiar as a pot plant indoors but outside it grows with vigour. Trained up a post it looks exactly like an evergreen tree with a cascading head providing beautiful long trails all the year round for large pedestal arrangements. Dense ivy always provides a welcome haven for the birds; it affords them a warm roosting place during the winter and nesting place in the spring.

There are numerous ivies to

choose from, among them: *Hedera helix*, 'Angularis Aurea' (yellow mottled with green), 'Buttercup' (bright yellow-green) and 'Goldheart' (dark green margined with a yellow heart-shaped centre). Another splendid variegated ivy is *H. h.* 'Cavendishii'. It is a 'must' for flower arrangers because of its thickly-clothed arborescent growth which produces masses of sweetly-scented tiny flowers followed by black fruits. Because of its growth pattern it is ideal for covering unsightly outdoor buildings as well as walls. Two more ivies which must be mentioned are *H. colchica* 'Dentata Variegata' which has large heart-shaped leaves splashed with yellow and a clone, 'Sulphur Heart', which has more variation in leaf colour. Ivies are wonderful plants for growing in urns and chimney pots as they cascade down the sides beautifully. They are ideal, too, in a winter hanging basket. Never take down your baskets as soon as the summer plants die off, fill them with ivies and some of the 'Universal' pansies which are available in a wide variety of colour and most accommodatingly, flower all winter long.

Viburnum Burkwoodii

All gardeners and arrangers alike, cherish the many evergreen shrubs which give us interestingly shaped and coloured leaves all year round. Among the favourites is *Fatsia japonica* with its wonderful palmate leaves of all sizes and its panicles of white globular flowers which usually appear in early winter. There is an attractive variegated form which is perhaps not as hardy as the green one. Another leathery-leaved tree, with lustrous yellow-green foliage is the *Griselinia littoralis*, but it needs to be planted in a sheltered spot.

But there are some evergreens which seem to thrive whatever the weather—like *Aucuba japonica* (variegata) (spotted laurel), *Buxus sempervirens* (box), *Choisya ternata* (Mexican orange), *Elaeagnus, Euonymus, Lonicera nitida* and *Skimmia japonica*. Another two never to be without because of their winter flowers are *Mahonia bealii* with its handsome foliage and its fragrant racemes of lemon-yellow flowers and *Viburnum tinus* (laurustinus). This shrub is of bushy habit

75

and can grow to a height of 3m, 10ft. The flowers have flat heads 5–10cms, 2–4ins across and are pink when in bud but white when fully open. There is also 'Variegatum' which, as one would expect, has very attractive golden variegated leaves. And speaking of viburnums, not to be forgotten are deciduous *V. fragrans* and *V. grandiflorum* or the hybrid × *bodnantense* with its pretty, sweetly scented flowers borne in clusters along the bare branches in the roughest months of winter—enough to gladden any heart.

Yellow is always a cheerful colour even more so during winter and no garden should be without the ever-popular winter–flowering jasmine (*Jasminum nudiflorum*), which seems to thrive anywhere, even on a cold sunless north wall. The *Hamamelis mollis* (Chinese witch–hazel) is another colourful and unusual shrub with its yellow spidery flowers clustered along bare branches. The winter flowers of the *Chimonanthus praecox* (winter sweet) are also yellow with purple inner petals and very sweet smelling. It grows best against a south or west wall where it can reach a height of 3m, 10ft. Some other

wall subjects which also flower in winter are two fragrant honeysuckles *Lonicera fragrantissima* and *L. standishii* and both have cream-white flowers. *Garrya elliptica*, sometimes nicknamed the tassel bush, is best grown against a wall although can be grown as a shrub in a sheltered spot. It is better to choose the male plant for planting as it bears 22cms, 8ins long grey catkins which look remarkably like clusters of caterpillars hanging from the stems! And although we think of *Clematis* as flowering in the milder months of the year, there are two with evergreen foliage which flower in mid-winter when given a sheltered southern aspect—*C. cirrhosa* and its cut-leafed variety *C. cirrhosa balearica*. Both have creamy-white small nodding flowers.

The hellebores, especially the green-flowering ones, are great favourites of the flower arranger, like the *Helleborus viridis*, *H. foetidus* and the *H. argutifolius* (= *H. corsicus*) which brighten up the winter garden for weeks on end. The first to open in the garden and which always gives untold pleasure is *H. atrorubens* with its stems of nodding cup-shaped plum-purple flowers with their striking yellow anthers. The Lenten rose *H. orientalis* is a variable plant and often produces flowers in shades of purple, pink and white. These plants grow well in the shrubbery where they get some protection from wind and frost. And even if you should find they have completely collapsed on a frosty morning, do not despair, by lunchtime they will have recovered and look as perky as ever. They like deep, well-drained but moist soil and hate to be disturbed. An annual top-dressing of leaf-mould as a mulch will keep them happy and flowering. The Christmas rose *H. niger* does not always live up to its name. Even when it is cosseted and covered with a cloche its beautiful fragile flowers do not usually appear until January. All these flowers are a delight for arranging although perhaps a little temperamental. You may cut a dozen and out of these two or three may flag regardless of the fact that they have all been treated in the same way; it is one of life's little mysteries! I leave the flowers until they are fully mature before cutting as they seem to last better at this stage. There

are those who say Christmas roses last better if the stems are pricked through with a needle before standing in deep water but success is not necessarily assured this way. All hellebores can be treated in the same way. First cut, put the ends of the stems in boiling water for a few seconds (taking care not to damage the flowers with the steam) and then stand them overnight up to their heads in water. Don't arrange them in floral foam or shallow water unless you are prepared to take them out of your arrangement each evening to stand overnight in deep water before arranging them again in the morning! My tip is just to enjoy them placed in a container which holds deep water like a specimen vase and hopefully you will have no problem.

Winter flowers, so precious and so few, can make the coldest winter day seem more like spring. Flowers like the winter aconite (*Eranthis hyemalis*) with its pale green leaves and lemon flowers along with the snowdrops (*Galanthus*) with their nodding white heads tipped with green are always a joy to behold. Both these plants are rather hard to establish in the garden and are best planted 'in the green'—a clump begged from a friend is usually the best bet.

The *Leucojum vernum* (snowflake) always reminds me of a tall snowdrop but on closer examination its flowers have a more rounded appearance with four or five nodding heads to a stem. Those exquisite tiny *Cyclamen coum* with their fascinating marbled leaves and their butterfly heads of pink, carmine and white are a delight but they, too, are rather hard to establish. Two more delightful winter treasures are the *Anemone blanda* with its small daisy-like flowers in shades of blue, mauve, pink and white and the early flowering *Crocus chrysanthus* and *C. tomasinianus*.

Here I must not forget that 'toughie', the Algerian iris, known to most of us as *I. stylosa* though it should strictly be referred to as *I. unguicularis*, its older botanical name. It thrives on neglect, with rich cultivation it produces more leaves and less flowers. Ideally, it prefers a poor gritty, limy soil in full sun when it will reward you with occasional flowers from before Christmas and into spring. It is best to pull the tightly rolled umbrella-like buds as they appear and take them indoors where they will quickly open to reveal their fragile beauty.

I have already mentioned a selection of favourite evergreens and here are a few flowering shrubs which will bring colour to your garden in winter. *Daphne mezereum* is one of the most popular early-flowering shrubs and rightly so as it can always be relied upon to give a splash of colour to cheer up any border. Flowers vary in colour from pale purple-pink to violet-red which are followed by scarlet berries, while the white form has yellow fruits. Two winter flowering rhododendrons are *R. dauricum* and *R. mucronulatum*. The evergreen *Sarcococca* has rather insignificant flowers but a delightful perfume. The Glastonbury thorn (*Crataegus monogyna* 'Biflora') often produces a second crop of flowers at this time of the year.

Trees that flower in the winter are few and far between but they always give pleasure. Perhaps the best known is *Prunus subhirtella* 'Autumnalis' (autumn cherry). It does, however, need a sheltered corner to escape the ravages of frost damage and if you are lucky you will be rewarded with a captivating display of semi-double white flowers for the grey winter days. 'Autumnalis Rosea' is similar but with pink flowers. *P. mume* (Japanese apricot) is another early-flowering species with the cultivars 'Alphandii' producing semi-double pink flowers and 'Beni-Shi-Don' which has perfumed rose-pink blooms in mid-February. *Cornus mas* (cornelian cherry) is not spectacular but its tiny pompom yellow flowers which appear along bare stems have a certain charm.

Another *Cornus* species which produces vivid coloured stems that shine brilliantly in the winter sunshine are well worth growing. Some good forms of *C. alba* are, 'Elegantissima', 'Sibirica' (= 'Westonbirt') and 'Spaethii'.

It is not only the coloured stems of shrubs that can add an extra dimension to the garden, there is a wide and fascinating array of trees with beautiful barks. They have all been given names which are totally descriptive of their appearance, like snakeskin, white washed, glossy, coloured and peeling. Three *Acer* species each with eye-catching barks, are *A. davidii* and *A. pensylvanicum* (both of these have green and white snakeskin-like barks) and *A. griseum* where its buff-coloured bark flakes off to reveal a bright and shining orange-brown colour beneath. Two white-barked trees are *Betula pendula* (silver birch) where the bark is both white and rough and *B. papyrifera* (paper birch) where on old trees the gleaming white bark peels away in large strips. *Prunus serrula* has a bark like polished mahogany while *Arbutus × andrachnoides* has a bark of pure cinnamon-red.

I have already mentioned the delight of viewing tree silhouettes against the sky and two favourites are well suited for this purpose. They are *Salix matsudana* 'Tortuosa' which will easily grow from a twig pushed into any damp spot. It is almost a case of pushing it in and standing back as growth is so quick. The other, *Corylus avellana* 'Contorta' (sometimes referred to as Harry Lauder's walking stick) is a very slow grower.

With flowers at a premium this is the time to gather just a few treasures for a tussy-mussy to enjoy indoors. The amount of pleasure they will give is totally out of proportion with their size. Small twigs from winter jasmine, autumn cherry and daphne along with a spray of the sweet-smelling flowers of mahonia, a few hellebores, snowdrops, *Iris unguicularis* and a few tiny ivy trails and marbled leaves from that wonderful plant *Arum italicum var. pictum*, would make a delightful perfumed arrangement.

Real gardeners never hibernate, they wrap up and carry on until the weather makes things impossible. Then they stay indoors to catch up on their reading of the latest gardening books and seed catalogues. But from time to time they'll gaze through the window and be rewarded with unexpected pleasures like watching visiting birds sometimes as colourful as any

flower, feed on the teasel and onopordum seedheads. With the snow come the more unusual visitors, so always make a point of leaving out suitable scraps and water for these unexpected callers.

Even in the harshest winter when plants seem devastated all is not always lost. You will find over the years that many plants have a terrific resilience and what at first seems completely dead often sends out fresh shoots when spring appears.

Let's face it—one has to be an optimist to be a gardener!

National Trust
Flower Gardens to Visit

Acorn Bank, Cumbria
Anglesey Abbey, Cambridgeshire
Antony House, Cornwall
Ardress House, Co Armagh
Arlington Court, Devon
Ascott, Buckinghamshire
Barrington Court, Somerset
Bateman's, East Sussex
Beningbrough Hall, North Yorkshire
Blickling Hall, Norfolk
Bodnant Garden, Gwynedd
Canons Ashby, Northamptonshire
Castle Drogo, Devon
Castle Ward, Co Down
Charlecote Park, Warwickshire
Chirk Castle, Clwyd
Clevedon Court, Avon
Cotehele, Cornwall
East Riddlesden Hall, West Yorkshire
Felbrigg Hall, Norfolk
Greys Court, Oxfordshire
Gunby Hall, Lincolnshire
Hardwick Hall, Derbyshire
Hidcote Manor Garden, Gloucestershire
Knightshayes Court, Devon
Lyme Park, Cheshire
Lytes Cary, Somerset

Melford Hall, Suffolk
Mompesson House, Wiltshire
Montacute House, Somerset
Mottisfont Abbey, Hampshire
Mount Stewart, Co Down
Overbecks, Devon
Owletts, Kent
Oxburgh Hall, Norfolk
Packwood House, Warwickshire
Peckover House, Cambridgeshire
Polesden Lacey, Surrey
Rowallane, Co Down
Rufford Old Hall, Lancashire
Saltram, Devon
Sizergh Castle, Cumbria
Snowshill Manor, Gloucestershire
Springhill, Co Londonderry
Standen, West Sussex
Trelissick, Cornwall
Trerice, Cornwall
Upton House, Warwickshire
The Vyne, Hampshire
Wakehurst Place, West Sussex
Wallington, Northumberland
Westbury Court Garden, Gloucestershire